LORD'S
The Guide

CONTENTS

Introduction

Welcome to Lord's, the home of cricket and of Marylebone Cricket Club (MCC).

This short guide is intended to complement your visit to Lord's, whether as a spectator or as a visitor on one of the popular Lord's tours.

The following pages will explore the history of this most famous of all cricket grounds, take you on a tour of its outstanding architecture, discover some of the great performances and explain the important role played by MCC in the world of cricket today.

We hope you enjoy your visit to the home of cricket and look forward to seeing you again soon.

Derek Underwood
MCC President 2008–09

MCC and its Role Today

Marylebone Cricket Club and Lord's

MCC can justly claim to be the most famous cricket club in the world. As the owner of Lord's, MCC is responsible for maintaining and developing cricket's most celebrated ground. It is also the custodian of the Laws of Cricket – since 1788 the Club has been responsible for any amendments to the Laws, a role it retains to this day. Furthermore, no other club is as active as MCC, which places huge emphasis on the development of the game all around the world and puts out men's and women's teams playing hundreds of fixtures every year.

Though MCC no longer oversees either the domestic or international game, the governing bodies still look to it for advice and assistance, most recently through the proposals that emerge from the MCC World Cricket committee.

In addition, MCC promotes an increasingly vigorous campaign entitled the 'Spirit of Cricket', which seeks to highlight the manner in which cricket is played and promote fair play and sportsmanship. The Spirit of Cricket is now enshrined in the Laws of the game.

Given its long and remarkable history, it is no surprise that MCC has the finest international collection of original art, books, manuscripts and other items relating to cricket. These cover not only the history of Lord's but also the development of the game worldwide. The highlight is the Ashes Urn, the single most famous object in cricket history.

Over the last two decades MCC has invested more than £40 million in various ground modernisation projects at Lord's, and this investment continues to ensure that Lord's has both a unique historical appeal and truly state-of-the-art sporting facilities.

The MCC monogram crowns the top of the Pavilion, 2004.

A panorama of Lord's, taken during the England v India Test match in 2002.

MCC Membership

Since its inception in 1787, MCC has remained a club focused on the development of cricket. It has a current membership of around 22,000. Members hail from all over the world and include men and women of all backgrounds linked by their love of the game.

Candidates must be aged at least 16 before being nominated, and there is a long waiting list: someone joining the list today could expect to wait 18 years before becoming a full member. It is possible, however, to become a Playing Member, and it is via this route that younger cricketers can become Members of MCC.

Many distinguished cricketers are honoured for their services to cricket by selection as Life Members or to honorary positions within the Club. Such figures include Richie Benaud, Sir Ian Botham, Sir Richard Hadlee, Sunil Gavaskar, Rachel Heyhoe-Flint and Nasser Hussain.

Cricket

During the course of a year MCC plays around 450 matches against schools and colleges, club and local sides as well as putting out first-class XIs to play against the counties or in representative matches. Women's teams account for an increasingly important part of MCC's cricket-playing programme. In 2008, 25 women's matches were played, including one against India. Additionally MCC undertakes a number of overseas tours each year by both men's and women's teams to nations as diverse as the Netherlands, Nigeria and Nepal in an effort to increase and encourage the development of cricket worldwide.

An MCC touring team in Japan lines up before Mount Fuji, September 2005.

An MCC team in action at Europa Point in Gibraltar in 2004. In the background is the Ibrahim-al-Ibrahim Mosque and the Rock of Gibraltar.

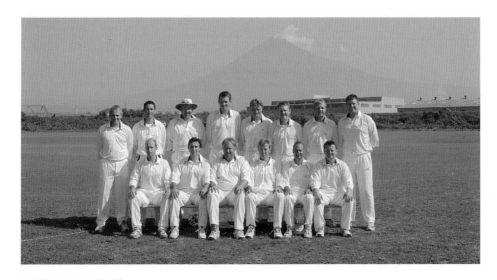

MCC Young Cricketers

The MCC Young Cricketers programme also demonstrates the Club's commitment to foster new talent. Each year some 20 talented young cricketers benefit from expert coaching, intensive playing programmes and world-class facilities at Lord's. The men compete in the County 2nd XI Championship. Many go on to win first-class contracts and sometimes even international caps. Famous 'graduates' of the Young Cricketers programme include Sir Ian Botham, Mark Waugh and Martin Crowe, and more recently Hamish Marshall and Caroline Atkins. Atkins is just one of several women MCC young cricketers who have gone on to represent England.

Mark Pettini (right), captain of Essex and an MCC Universities graduate, and Ryan ten Doeschate (left) lift the Friends Provident Trophy at Lord's after Essex had defeated Kent in the 2008 final at Lord's.

University Cricket

Since 2005, MCC has taken responsibility for the development and funding of the University Centres of Cricketing Excellence. In his foreword to the MCC Universities prospectus, Tony Lewis, Chairman of MCC World Cricket committee, explains the scheme:

> Many people dream of a career playing their chosen sport but this often means leaving behind their academic studies. MCC Universities offer you the chance to pursue your cricket career without compromising your education. Indeed the six specialist centres – Cambridge, Cardiff/Glamorgan, Durham, Leeds/Bradford, Loughborough and Oxford – combine state of the art facilities, exceptional coaching and technical back-

up developed specifically with cricket in mind. Some may scorn the academic half of this deal. We should remember, though, the wisdom of the great West Indian CLR James who famously wrote: 'What do they know of cricket who only cricket know?'

MCC Universities graduates include Andrew Strauss, Monty Panesar, Nicki Shaw, James Foster, Mark Pettini and Jamie Dalrymple.

The Laws of Cricket and MCC World Cricket Committee

MCC published its first revised code of Laws in 1788, just one year after the Club was founded. Since then it has retained the guardianship of the Laws of Cricket. The most recent revision, known as the 2000 Code 3rd Edition, was published in 2008. This update particularly addressed the materials of the bat, in response to innovations by manufacturers. Approved by MCC Members on 1st October 2008, the revised code is authorised for use in all competitions and is available in a large number of languages from Bahasa to Japanese.

ICC match officials at Lord's: match referee Roshan Mahanama and umpires Steve Davis, Nigel Llong, Daryl Harper and Rudi Koertzen.

As an adjunct to its custodianship of the Laws, and as a think-tank for those at the heart of the game, in April 2006 MCC established a World Cricket committee. It is the only truly independent voice in world cricket, free from considerations of

Members of the MCC World Cricket committee assembled at Lord's in May 2008. STANDING: Barry Richards, Mike Atherton, Tony Dodemaide, Courtney Walsh, David Richardson, Geoffrey Boycott, Alec Stewart, Mike Gatting. SEATED: Steve Waugh, Mike Brearley, Tony Lewis (chairman), David Shepherd, Majid Khan, Andy Flower.

Rahul Dravid, Shaun Pollock and Anil Kumble in October 2008, wearing MCC ties presented to them on their election as MCC Honorary Life Members. The three have recently become members of the MCC World Cricket committee.

money, politics and nationality and is composed of current and former international cricketers and umpires from across the globe. Meeting twice yearly to discuss the prevalent issues in the game, it acts as a complementary body to the International Cricket Council (ICC) and its constituent nations.

MCC World Cricket committee is empowered to conduct research, particularly into technological advances and bio-mechanical elements of the game and its players. MCC supports this work with its increasing investment into research and development. The aims of the committee are:

to debate all matters in the interests of cricket and cricketers; to consider at all times the balance of the contest between bat and ball and to assist MCC's custodianship of the Laws of the game; to protect the Spirit of Cricket; and to be sure that governing body decisions never put cash or country interests before the good of the game.

The committee's debates and decisions are made solely in the interest of cricket and its players.

The Spirit of Cricket

Former England fast bowler David 'Syd' Lawrence coaching a boy on one of MCC's Spirit of Cricket camps.

MCC has long believed that cricket should be played, not just within the Laws, but also in accordance within the game's traditional 'spirit'. In the late 1990s two distinguished MCC Members (and ex-England captains), Ted Dexter and Lord Cowdrey, sought to enshrine the 'Spirit of Cricket' in the game's Laws in order to remind players of their responsibility for ensuring that cricket is always played in a sportsmanlike manner. All new codes of Laws now include a preamble on the 'Spirit of Cricket', which explains the roles and responsibilities of captains, players and umpires in respecting and upholding the Spirit of Cricket.

MCC promotes the Spirit of Cricket both in Britain and overseas through grassroots cricket initiatives and partnerships with cricket organisations such as the Indian Premier League and *Chance to Shine*. Events include the annual Cowdrey Lecture, which is given at Lord's by a distinguished figure. Speakers have included Sir Clive Lloyd, Barry Richards, Geoffrey Boycott, Christopher Martin-Jenkins and, most recently, Archbishop Desmond Tutu. In addition many current and recent international cricketers such as Andrew Flintoff, Rahul Dravid and Brett Lee have thrown their weight behind MCC's initiative.

Archbishop Desmond Tutu giving the 2008 Cowdrey Lecture.

Community Relations

MCC plays an active role in the life of the local community in the area around Lord's. Local residents are invited to attend summer open days at Lord's; local schoolchildren are invited to attend matches; and MCC stages an annual carol concert for the community, with proceeds going to a local charity. MCC also works closely with the London Schools Cricket Association, which is able to make use of the Indoor School facilities throughout the year.

The ICC, the ECB and Middlesex CCC

Lord's is not only home to MCC but also to other important bodies, whose presence at Lord's has long added to the importance of Lord's as a centre of cricket.

The Imperial Cricket Conference was founded at Lord's in 1909 by representatives from England, Australia and South Africa. In 1926 India, New Zealand and the West Indies were elected as full members. They were joined by Pakistan in 1953, Sri Lanka in 1981, Zimbabwe in 1992 and Bangladesh in 2000. South Africa ceased to be a member on leaving the British Commonwealth in 1961, but was re-elected as a full member in 1991.

In 1989 the ICC, by now known as the International Cricket

Afternoon sunshine during the 1995 Natwest Final, in which Warwickshire beat Northamptonshire.

Council, adopted a new set of rules and became a legislative body where binding decisions could be taken for the management of international cricket. The expansion of cricket, especially in the Indian subcontinent, has vastly increased the responsibilities of the ICC, which is now the governing body for international cricket. In August 2005 the ICC moved its offices away from St John's Wood to centralise all its operations in Dubai, sadly bringing to an end the ICC's 96-year association with Lord's.

The England and Wales Cricket Board (ECB) is the governing body of cricket in England and Wales. It was established in 1997 and took over the responsibilities carried out for the previous 30 years by the Test and County Cricket Board, the National Cricket Association and the Cricket Council. Its stated aim is to ensure that England becomes and remains the most successful and respected cricket nation in the world, and to encourage the widest possible participation and interest in the game throughout England and Wales. The ECB is responsible for the administration of international cricket in England and the England team. It also manages England tours overseas.

Middlesex playing Derbyshire in a Natwest Pro40 match at Lord's on 10th September 2007 – the first match played under floodlights at Lord's.

At the head of the ECB is a management board headed by an elected chairman. Below that are two representative bodies. The First Class Forum comprises all 18 first class counties and MCC, and decides all aspects of domestic and international cricket. The Recreational Forum covers school, club, league and inter-county

cricket in the non-first class game.

Middlesex County Cricket Club has been playing its county fixtures at Lord's since 1877. The club's administrative offices and shop are also based at Lord's, and Middlesex has its own clubroom in the lower tier of the Allen Stand. On Middlesex match days, members of the county are able to use the facilities of the Lord's Pavilion – becoming a Middlesex member is one way of watching cricket from the Pavilion without waiting 18 years to become a member of MCC.

Middlesex also plays home fixtures at grounds in Southgate, Uxbridge and Richmond and runs an academy for young cricketers at the Finchley Indoor School in north London.

The Colours of MCC

There has always been debate about the origin of the MCC colours. The Club played in light blue until the 1860s, when the famous red and gold appeared for the first time. The Museum houses a boundary flag, dating from this period, which is the earliest known example of the red and gold logo.

The colours are similar to those used as racing colours by the Duke of Richmond. One of the current Duke's ancestors was very much involved in the early days of MCC, but it is unlikely that MCC would have chosen to take on his colours some 80 years after the Club's foundation.

It has also been suggested that MCC borrowed their colours from I Zingari, the first and grandest of the wandering clubs to be founded in the mid-1800s. I Zingari's colours were black, red and gold, reflecting their motto, 'out of darkness, through fire, into light'.

MCC team selected to play Sussex, the previous season's Champion County, in 2007's season-opening fixture at Lord's, all wearing their MCC sweaters with the famous red and yellow. STANDING: Zoheb Sharif, Tim Bresnan, Alex Gidman, Graham Onions, Nick Compton, Alex Loudon, Steven Davies, Adil Rashid. SEATED: Owais Shah, Matthew Hoggard, Alastair Cook (captain), Steve Harmison.

The founders of I Zingari: Sir Spencer Ponsonby-Fane, JL Baldwin and Lord Bessborough, painted by Lowes Cato Dickinson. Sir Spencer was the founding father of MCC's Museum collections.

The MCC flag flying above the Grand Stand.

Many members of I Zingari would also have been members of MCC, but it is doubtful whether MCC – a distinguished club of almost 100 years standing at that time – would have borrowed its colours from a club only a few years old, no matter how grand the latter was.

In 1866, when MCC had the chance to purchase the freehold of Lord's Ground, the money required was advanced by one the Club's Members, William Nicholson. Without this advance it is likely that the Ground would have been sold to a property developer and MCC's future would have been very much in doubt. Nicholson continued to loan the Club substantial amounts for numerous projects over the next 30 years and was President of MCC in 1879.

William Nicholson was the owner of the Nicholson's Gin Company, the colours of which were red and yellow. Although no written proof has yet been found, there is a strong family tradition that the adoption of the red and gold was MCC's personal thank you to William Nicholson for his services to the Club – sport's first corporate sponsorship deal, perhaps? In Victorian England such commercial deals would have been frowned upon, but there is a strong possibility that the adoption of these colours was a nice way of acknowledging Nicholson's huge contribution towards assuring the future of MCC.

Whatever their origin, there is no doubt that MCC's red and gold are among the most famous club colours in sport and are instantly recognised around the world.

A Treasure House

The MCC Museum, Library and Archive

In 1864 MCC owned only two pictures. A senior member of the Club, Sir Spencer Ponsonby-Fane, persuaded the Committee to make a general request for items of cricketing interest that might enhance the appearance of the Pavilion. It was a labour of love for Sir Spencer to look out for items as they came up for auction and to persuade the Committee to purchase them. Thus began what has become one of the sporting world's most important historic collections.

In 1953 His Royal Highness the Duke of Edinburgh opened what was then known as the Memorial Gallery, and has since become the MCC Museum. The Duke is a keen follower of the game and the only person to have held the position of MCC President on two occasions (in 1949 and 1974), and MCC was delighted that he was able to attend celebrations for the Museum's golden jubilee in 2003.

At the latest count, the Museum's holdings numbered around 30,000 items, which are housed primarily in the Library, Museum and Archive, though displays are mounted throughout the Ground at different times of the year. Together, they provide an amazing all-round resource for those interested in the game, and MCC welcomes enquiries from members of the public as well as researchers, authors, historians

Portrait by R Hannaford of Sir Donald Bradman, acclaimed as the greatest batsman of all time.

Display case in the MCC Museum showing items relating to Victor Trumper, one of the greatest Australian batsmen of all, renowned for his ability on a sticky wicket.

Portrait of Muttiah Muralitharan by the London-based American artist Phil Hale. The painting was commissioned as part of MCC's Lord's Portrait Project and unveiled in 2007 on the day the great Sri Lankan bowler became the world record holder for Test wickets taken.

The MCC Museum in 2005, with an exhibition of Patrick Eagar's photographs at Lord's on display upstairs.

and, of course, Members of MCC. A daily tour programme allows visitors a detailed look at not only the collections, but also the fascinating architecture around the Ground.

There is presently a lengthy project to re-catalogue and conserve the collections, and MCC also has an active programme for recording important cricketing events and records as they are created and for commemorating the players who achieved them.

A 1993 conversation piece by Andrew Festing, depicting England cricketers from the 1970s and 1980s. FROM LEFT TO RIGHT: John Emburey, Graham Gooch, David Gower, Mike Gatting, Tony Greig, Bob Taylor, Allan Lamb, Mike Brearley, Bob Willis and Derek Randall. Stephen Green, the Club's curator for over 30 years, is seated in the background.

Lewis Cage: The Young Cricketer by Sir Francis Cotes (1768) – arguably the greatest cricketing portrait of the 18th century, and recently acquired by MCC.

Memorabilia is actively sought, and portraits are commissioned each year to celebrate key figures in the cricketing world. Recent commissions have included highly acclaimed paintings, drawings, photographs and sculptures of figures such as Shane Warne, Sachin Tendulkar, Sir Vivian Richards and John Woodcock. An oral history project has recorded interviews with many famous personalities in the game, including two fascinating series in India and Sri Lanka.

Through a series of annual exhibitions, MCC has presented and interpreted events and the collections at Lord's, working with figures such as Patrick Eagar, perhaps the most respected photographer of the game (many of whose photographs you will see in this guide), Brian Lara and others. Furthermore, through sponsorship of young artists and photographers, MCC has sought to allow them in turn to depict and interpret cricket at Lord's and in every Test playing nation.

The most ambitious project attempted in recent years was the Ashes Exhibition in Australia in 2006–07. Undoubtedly the most famous object in the collection, the Urn was exhibited in seven locations over 14 weeks and was viewed by over 100,000 visitors. Its popularity attests to its fascinating and often misunderstood history.

The MCC Library contains the world's largest and most comprehensive collection of books and publications dedicated to cricket. Spanning over 11,000 volumes, from the latest books and magazines to rare editions and pamphlets from the game's earliest days, the Library is an invaluable resource for authors, researchers and journalists. As well as a complete set of Wisden Cricketers' Almanack, the collection also includes the only known complete set of *Britcher's Scores* and many other items of a rare and precious nature. Many works on other bat and ball games are also featured in the collection, most notably on Real Tennis, a sport with which MCC has a long association.

The size and diversity of the collection is reflected in the range of research which takes place in the Library. Undergraduate students researching popular topics such as the 'Bodyline' series may find themselves sharing the Library with textile designers

Sir Garfield Sobers having his portrait painted by Sarah Raphael during the 1992 England v Pakistan Test.

Books in the MCC Library, including volumes of James Lillywhite's *Cricketers' Annual* from the 1890s.

looking into the history of cricket costume or even prominent authors researching their next work. Among the many books to have relied upon research carried out in the Library are Sir John Major's history of cricket *More Than a Game* and Peter Oborne's *Basil D'Oliveira: Cricket and Conspiracy, the Untold Story*.

The collection is currently growing at a rate of approximately 400 volumes per year with new items arriving from all over the world covering all aspects of the game and its history. The MCC Library is open to researchers on non-match days throughout the year. On match days it operates as a private Club Library offering MCC Members a relaxed and comfortable environment in which to read during breaks in play.

Lord's on a Gentlemen v Players day, by Lowes Cato Dickinson (19th century).

Display case in the Museum showing memorabilia from the infamous 1932–33 'Bodyline' Ashes series in Australia.

Shane Warne unveils his portrait, painted by artist Fanny Rush (right) in 2005. During that summer's Ashes Test at Lord's, Warne became the first cricketer to walk past a portrait of himself in the Long Room during a Test match in which he was playing.

The original scorebook from the 1882 England v Australia Test at the Oval, the match that was the origin of the Ashes.

The Ashes Urn

Standing only 4in (about 10cm) high and made of terracotta, the Ashes Urn has come to be recognised as the most famous symbol of sporting rivalry.

The story begins on 29th August 1882, at the Kennington Oval when Australia narrowly defeated a strong England side in what remains one of the most dramatic Test matches ever played. This first Australian victory on English soil was considered a national calamity and the following day a mock obituary notice appeared in the *Sporting Times*, which lamented the death of English Cricket at the Oval, and announced that 'the body will be cremated and the ashes taken to Australia'.

Photograph of the 1882 Oval Test in progress.

The Ashes Urn and the velvet bag presented to Ivo Bligh.

The mock obituary notice that appeared in the *Sporting Times*.

In Affectionate Remembrance

OF

ENGLISH CRICKET,

WHICH DIED AT THE OVAL

ON

29th AUGUST, 1882,

Deeply lamented by a large circle of sorrowing friends and acquaintances.

R.I.P.

N.B.—The body will be cremated and the ashes taken to Australia.

This reference was particularly topical as the legal status of cremation was then of much public debate, which perhaps explains why the idea captured people's imagination so vividly. It was clearly still at the forefront of the sporting public's mind when the challenge of the following series was taken up by the Hon. Ivo Bligh (later Lord Darnley); he set off for Australia vowing 'to recover the ashes'.

The idea was rekindled again in Australia with references made during various speeches during the tour until Christmas Eve, when Ivo Bligh and the other amateur members of his side were invited to stay at the home of Sir William Clarke, president of the Melbourne Club and the sponsor of the tour. The Englishmen played a game against the estate staff and at the conclusion of the match it seems that Lady Clarke arranged for a bail to be burned and deposited in a small 'urn' – the original Ashes Urn. To much amusement, she presented this to Ivo Bligh, announcing that here at last were the Ashes which he had come so far to regain. The Test series began after Christmas, and when England won the series Lady Clarke added to the Urn two small paper labels, one of them containing a rhyme clipped from the *Melbourne Punch* predicting the triumphant return of England. Finally one of Lady Clarke's friends presented Bligh with a velvet bag in which to carry the Urn, and he returned to

The England team that travelled to Australia in 1882–83 'to recover the Ashes'.
BACK ROW: W Barnes, F Morley, CT Studd, GF Vernon, CFH Leslie.
MIDDLE ROW: GB Studd, EFS Tylecote, The Hon. Ivo Bligh, AG Steel, WW Read.
FRONT ROW: RG Barlow, W Bates.

England with his prize.

He continued to treasure the Urn and bag as personal gifts and kept them at his family home, Cobham Hall near Rochester in Kent, until his death in 1927, when his widow presented the Urn to MCC in recognition of its growing importance to cricket.

The idea of the Ashes has been associated with the Anglo-Australian rivalry ever since. Indeed from 1903–04, when it fell to MCC to organise the tours to and from Australia, the word 'Ashes' was used in reference to each series. It is clear, though, from the variety of illustrations to the publications, that there was no knowledge of the Urn itself. Ivo Bligh must nevertheless have realised that his gift had been the first physical embodiment of this idea and consequently bequeathed it to the headquarters of English cricket.

X-ray of the Urn taken in 2002, showing the pin used to repair the Urn before it ever arrived at Lord's.

The Ashes Urn alongside the glass trophy that is now presented to the winners of each Ashes series.

Australian domination of series in the late 1980s and 1990s, combined with a vogue for 'trophies', gave rise to calls from Australia for the Urn to be presented as a trophy. MCC declined, citing its history as a reason against such a use. Instead, after discussions with the England and Wales Cricket Board (ECB) and Cricket Australia, MCC commissioned from Waterford Crystal a glass trophy in the form of the Urn. This was first presented to Mark Taylor in 1998/99, and is now presented at the end of each Ashes series to be retained by the victors.

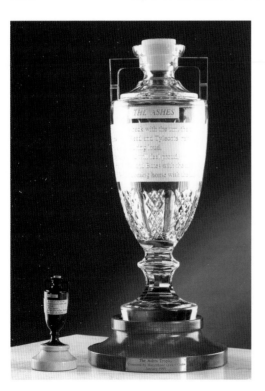

In 2002, X-rays revealed that the Urn had been badly damaged in a fall prior to its arrival at Lord's and that repairs carried out at the time had become unstable. This lent credence to a Darnley family story that a maid at Cobham Hall had knocked the Urn from the mantelpiece. Not only did this prevent the Urn travelling to Australia in 2002, but it also raised questions as to why Lord Darnley had had an insignificant little urn repaired with such care. Some suggest that it had come to symbolise the start of his courtship with his wife, Lady Florence, who had started life as Florence Rose Morphy and whom he had met when she was governess of the Clarke household on Christmas Eve 1882.

Further conservation of the Urn was completed in 2004 and it was flown to Australia for the exhibition in 2006–07. It is now back on display at Lord's.

The Honours Boards

By scoring a century or taking five wickets in an innings, a player ensures that his name is added to one of the famous Honours Boards in the Pavilion. These boards, situated in the home and away dressing rooms, provide a permanent reminder of the best batting and bowling performances in the long history of Lord's. The names speak for themselves, evoking memories of great matches and great players.

Only one cricketer has the distinction of appearing on the Honours Boards in both dressing rooms. Gordon Greenidge made centuries for the West Indies against England in 1984 and 1988. He also made a century whilst representing MCC in the 1987 Bicentenary Match against a Rest of the World XI, which placed him in the home dressing room too.

It is also unusual for a player to appear in both the lists for batting and bowling. Only the great all-rounders Sir Garfield Sobers, Keith Miller, MH 'Vinoo' Mankad and Sir Ian Botham have achieved this feat.

Of equal interest is a list of top cricketers who did not make the list. Michael Atherton was run out on 99 against Australia in 1993, and the names of Dennis Lillee, Imran Khan, Brian Lara and Sachin Tendulkar are also missing from the boards.

The Honours Board recording the best Test match bowling performances at Lord's for England is located in the home dressing room.

Shivnarine Chanderpaul (West Indies) in the away dressing room in 2004, in front of the Honours Board that bears his name.

Top ten Test match performances at Lord's: batting (* = not out)

333	GA Gooch	England v India	1990
259	GC Smith	South Africa v England	2003
254	DG Bradman	Australia v England	1930
221	RWT Key	England v West Indies	2004
214*	CG Greenidge	West Indies v England	1984
211	JB Hobbs	England v South Africa	1924
208	DCS Compton	England v South Africa	1947
206*	WA Brown	Australia v England	1938
206	MP Donnelly	New Zealand v England	1949
205*	J Hardstaff jnr	England v India	1946

Highest centuries for other countries

200	Mohsin Khan	Pakistan v England	1982
190	S Wettimuny	Sri Lanka v England	1984
184	MH Mankad	India v England	1952

Top ten Test match performances at Lord's: bowling

8-34	IT Botham	England v Pakistan	1978
8-38	GD McGrath	Australia v England	1997
8-43	H Verity	England v Australia	1934
8-51	DL Underwood	England v Pakistan	1974
8-53	RAL Massie	Australia v England	1972
8-84	RAL Massie	Australia v England	1972
8-103	IT Botham	England v West Indies	1984
7-32	DL Underwood	England v New Zealand	1969
7-36	G Ulyett	England v Australia	1884
7-39	JB Statham	England v South Africa	1955

Best bowling for other countries (5 wickets or better)

7-65	SJ Pegler	South Africa v England	1912
6-32	Mudassar Nazar	Pakistan v England	1982
6-32	MD Marshall	West Indies v England	1988
6-35	L Amar Singh	India v England	1936
6-76	DJ Nash	New Zealand v England	1994
6-87	RJ Ratnayake	Sri Lanka v England	1991
5-69	HH Streak	Zimbabwe v England	2000

The Origins and Early History of Cricket

The origins of cricket are uncertain but the game is of great antiquity. The earliest surviving reference is found in the Guildford Borough Archives in Surrey and states that that the game was played at the Free Grammar School in Guildford in around 1550.

As one of a number of English folk games played with a bat and ball, cricket was particularly popular in the south-east corner of England among the sheep-farming communities of the Weald of Kent and Sussex. Nobility visiting their country estates noticed their servants and tenants playing the game and realised that, as well as being an entertaining pastime, cricket would provide an excellent means of a wager – England in the early 18th century was betting mad. Members of the gentry began to form their own teams and the stakes on some of the matches were so high, sometimes as much as 1000 guineas, that it was necessary to know that both sides were playing to the same rules.

In 1727 'Articles of Agreement' governing the conduct of matches were drawn up between the Duke of Richmond and a Mr Broderick; they appear to be a supplement to a code of Laws, dated 1722, that no longer exists. The earliest surviving issue of the Laws of Cricket dates from 1744 and can be seen printed around the edge of a handkerchief that is on display in the MCC Museum.

For a while the leading cricket club was Hambledon in Hampshire, but as the gentry began to spend more time at court in London the centre of the game shifted to the capital.

A detail from *Cricket in Marylebone Fields*, painted by Francis Hayman (c.1740). Though the location is disputed, it is universally acknowledged as the most accurate pictorial description of 18th-century cricket.

The first Lord's ground, as depicted in 1793.

Lord of Lord's

One of the leading London clubs was the White Conduit in Islington, an exclusive club patronised by many of the finest gentlemen of the day including George Finch, the 9th Earl of Winchilsea. The gentlemen of the White Conduit wanted a ground much nearer to central London and in 1786 Winchilsea approached a young man who was employed as a general attendant and ground bowler at the club. 'Establish a private ground,' he suggested, 'and we will ensure against any financial loss.' The man's name was Thomas Lord.

Thomas Lord was an ambitious Yorkshireman who had come to London to remake the family fortune lost during the Jacobite Rebellion. He was an astute businessman who, in addition to working at the White Conduit Club, also ran a wine merchant's. Lord was a capable cricketer, but it was his business instinct that really recommended him to Winchilsea and his associates. Lord was quick to seize the opportunity. He obtained a lease on part of the Portman family estate in the area then known as Dorset Fields, erected a high wooden fence, and built a hut for cricketers to store their equipment in. The first recorded encounter on Lord's new ground took place on 31st May 1787 between teams representing Middlesex and Essex. The prize money was 100 guineas.

Thomas Lord's ground proved popular with the members of the White Conduit Club, who were soon calling themselves the Marylebone Club in reference to their geographical location. Soon the Marylebone Cricket Club had taken over from Hambledon the task of revising the Laws of Cricket and, by the turn of the century, had become London's leading club. Today, more than 200 years later, MCC remains the body responsible for the Laws of the game worldwide.

In 1805 Lord's hosted its first ever Eton v Harrow match. In 2005 this annual match celebrated its 200th anniversary. It is the only surviving fixture from the original Lord's Ground.

London was expanding rapidly and rents were rising. When the lease on Dorset Fields expired in 1811, Thomas Lord refused to pay the rent increase and closed the ground. He had the foresight, however, to rent a couple of fields on the Eyre family estate in rural St John's Wood for £54 per annum. Lord moved everything, including his turf, to the new ground, which was officially opened on 8th May 1811. The ground was not popular with Members of MCC – in fact the Club did not play a single match there in 1811 or 1812. So it was with no great concern that Lord learned in 1812 that

A portrait of Thomas Lord, c. 1810; the artist is unknown but the picture was donated to Lord's by Florence Lord, a direct descendent of Thomas.

Above and below: Two sketches by George Shepherd (1770–1842), showing Thomas Lord in action.

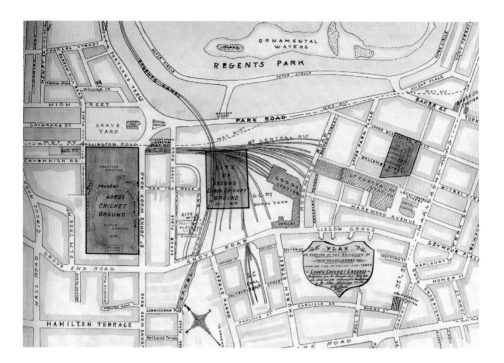

A 1902 map showing the position of Thomas Lord's three grounds.

Andrew Strauss, of Middlesex and England, at the site of the second Lord's ground.

Parliament intended to cut the new Regent's Canal right through the ground. In fact he managed to turn the situation to his advantage. He made firm representations to the Eyre estate, who gave him £4,000 compensation and found him another plot in St John's Wood at a rent of £100 per annum. Lord moved his turf a second time and erected a pavilion and tavern on the premises. The first match at Lord's new ground took place on 22nd June 1814, when MCC beat Hertfordshire by an innings and 27 runs.

It looked as if MCC now had a permanent home in St John's Wood. However, Thomas Lord was, first and foremost, a businessman. There can be little doubt that it was his business brain that ruled over any fondness he had for his cricketing tenants. Although now almost 70 years old, he fancied one last business speculation and in 1825 shocked MCC with the announcement that he had permission from the Eyre estate to develop houses on part of the outfield – only 150 square yards would have remained for cricket.

MCC was saved by one of its Members, William Ward, a director of the Bank of England and MP for the City of London. He was particularly fond of Lord's, having scored 278 runs for MCC v Norfolk in 1820 – the highest score in any class of cricket at that time, and a ground record that survived almost a century. The match ball can be seen in the MCC Museum. Ward was horrified by Lord's proposal. He asked how much Lord wanted for the lease, and

on the spot wrote a cheque for £5,000. Thus Lord's was saved from the property developers.

Disaster struck almost immediately when on 29th July the Pavilion burnt down – taking with it all of the Club's early records. However, the speed with which a new Pavilion was built – it was ready in time for the anniversary dinner in May 1826 – proved that Lord's was in safe hands.

In 1835 William Ward transferred the lease of Lord's to JH Dark. Dark was the son of a saddler, born in the Edgware Road. At the age of ten, he had begun what was to be a 60-year association with Lord's when he earned pocket money as a fielder at Lord's original ground in Dorset Fields.

The ground that Dark inherited was very much a rural one – more like a field than a grand cricket pitch. Sheep were used to keep the grass short. In fact, for many years the Lord's pitch was notorious for being one of the worst in England – a surface not at all favoured by batsmen having to face the new, faster round-arm bowling technique being introduced into the game at the time.

Dark did not find it easy to make money out of cricket. Between 1830 and 1863 there were never more than 23 matches played at Lord's in a year – sometimes as few as nine. Dark supplemented his income by using Lord's as a showground for a number of unusual events, including an encampment of the Ioway Indians who put on displays of dancing and archery. He was, however, a loyal supporter of MCC and ploughed much of his profit back into the facilities in the hope of encouraging the expansion of the Club.

In 1838 he constructed a Tennis court on the site of the current Mound Stand. It included hot and cold baths and a billiard table for Members to use after their Tennis game. The following year a scoring perch was erected that allowed the match scorer an uninterrupted view of play. In 1842 he made a running track around the Ground. This was well used by the Members and was also used to promote events such as pony racing, hurdle races and stone-picking contests – all popular with the general public. A racquets court was added in 1844.

A watercolour of Lord's in 1837, depicting the Grand Jubilee Match held between the North and South of England to mark MCC's 50th anniversary.

John Wisden, by W Bromley. Wisden was the founder of the famous cricketing almanack that bears his name to this day.

The Age of Grace

Despite Dark's improvements, MCC still struggled to maintain its match schedule. Many cricketers preferred the flatter turf at the Oval. MCC was in decline. In 1860 the Club did not even bid for the freehold of the Ground, which was sold by the Eyre estate to a Mr Moses for £7,000. Moses then approached Dark with an offer to purchase the leasehold of Lord's – with both, he would have been able to develop the Ground for housing. Dark was nearly 70 and, had he accepted the offer, it would have been the end of Lord's and possibly MCC. But Dark remained loyal. He refused to sell to Moses and offered instead first refusal on his interest in Lord's to MCC.

The Committee responded positively. The Club's first full-time secretary, RA Fitzgerald, immediately set about negotiating terms for the purchase of the lease. At the AGM in 1864 MCC agreed unanimously to purchase Dark's interest in the Ground for £11,000 plus £1,500 for fixtures and fittings. This would be raised via a voluntary donation fund and by creating a number of life memberships at £300 each. MCC also negotiated a new 99-year lease with Mr Moses – so for the immediate future at least the Club was safe.

The advantages enjoyed by MCC in owning the leasehold of Lord's prompted Fitzgerald to suggest that MCC approach Mr Moses with a view to securing the freehold of Lord's. Moses made MCC pay dearly for its failure to bid in 1860: they paid £18,333 6s 8d for the freehold, three times the price he had paid only six years before. MCC was once again fortunate in its benefactors, and on this occasion the money for the purchase was raised thanks to an influential member, William Nicholson, who offered to advance the sum on a mortgage of the premises.

MCC was now fully able to call Lord's its own. In order to attract new members it had to transform the Ground into one fitting for cricket's foremost club. Progress was rapid on and off the field. The first Grand Stand (1866–67) and the famous Tavern (1867–68) were built. The 1868 season saw an Australian aboriginal side play at Lord's. During the lunch break they demonstrated their skills with various hunting weapons, of which a *nulla nulla* is still on display in the MCC Museum. Also in 1868, in the Gentlemen v Players match (an annual fixture which had been held since 1806 between the leading amateur and professional cricketers), a 19-year-old from Gloucestershire called WG Grace scored a brilliant century, making

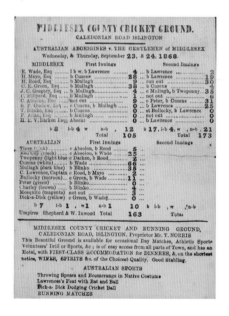

Scorecard from the MCC Archives, detailing a match that took place in 1868 between the touring team of Australian Aboriginal cricketers and the Gentlemen of Middlesex, held at the nearby ground on Caledonian Road.

his first mark on the game that he would dominate for the next 40 years. In the same year Fitzgerald's appointment as Secretary became a paid one, with a salary of £400 a year. In 1872 he took a strong amateur touring team to North America.

MCC's programme of work continued throughout the 1870s and 1880s. By the spring of 1874 the great work of raising and re-levelling the playing area was complete. The benefits were immediately apparent. The ground soon lost its reputation of having the most dangerous pitch in the country, and instead MCC was able to offer one of England's finest playing surfaces – alongside its unmatched facilities.

In 1876 Henry Perkins, a barrister and journalist, became MCC Secretary. The following year Middlesex first played at Lord's and began its long association with the Ground.

MCC was surprisingly slow to stage Test cricket. The first England v Australia Test was played at Melbourne in 1877, but the first home international fixtures were held at the Oval (in 1880 and 1882) and Old Trafford (1884). Lord's staged its inaugural Test on 21st–23rd July 1884. England beat Australia by an innings.

In 1887 the Club celebrated its centenary and at the AGM that year the Committee were pleased to report that MCC was flourishing. The centenary was celebrated by the purchase of

An 1891 photograph of Fred 'The Demon' Spofforth, the legendary Australian fast bowler who terrorised English batsmen in the 1870s and 1880s. Without him the Ashes might never have existed, for he took 14 wickets in the famous 1882 Oval Test in which Australia defeated England.

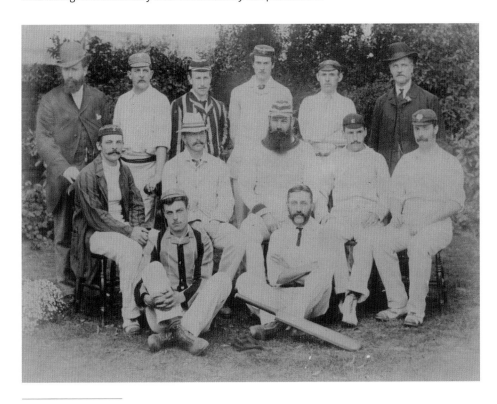

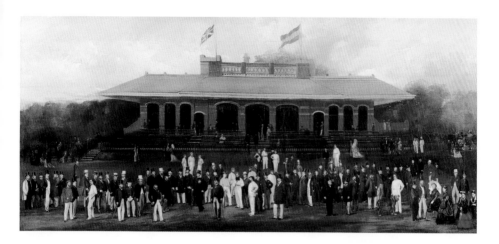

The Lord's Pavilion (1874), by LH Barraud. In 1890 this building was superseded by the present Pavilion.

The England team that played Australia in the first ever Test match at Lord's, 21st–23rd July 1884.
BACK ROW:
CK Pullin (umpire), E Peate, AP Lucas, Hon. A Lyttelton, A Shrewsbury, FH Farrands (umpire).
MIDDLE ROW:
AG Steel, Lord Harris, WG Grace, WW Read, G Ulyett.
FRONT ROW:
S Christopherson, RG Barlow.

Henderson's Nursery for the sum of £18,500. This three-and-a-half-acre site had been a market garden famous for its pineapples and tulips. Its purchase enabled MCC to lay a separate practice area. The name 'Nursery End' stuck, although today the association is made more readily with the nurturing of young cricketers rather than fruit and flowers. In 1890 the new Pavilion was opened. This is now the oldest existing building at Lord's.

In 1891 MCC faced a crisis when the Manchester and Sheffield Railway wanted to cut across the Nursery Ground in order to extend their line into Marylebone. Henry Perkins saved the day by suggesting a compromise. MCC acquired the site of the Clergy Female Orphan School from the railway in exchange for permission to tunnel under the practice ground.

This was Perkins's finest hour. In 1898 Francis Lacey, the first cricketer to be knighted for services to the game, succeeded him. During his time the first Mound Stand was built and two important bodies met for the first time at Lord's – the Advisory County Cricket Committee in 1904, and the Imperial Cricket Conference (forerunner of the International Cricket Council) in 1909. In 1903–04 MCC sent its first official overseas side to Australia. For the next 70 years MCC was to oversee all England tours abroad. The 1903–04 side was led by 'Plum' (later Sir Pelham) Warner, a great cricketer and administrator who would be a doyen of MCC until the 1960s.

In just over 100 years, Lord's had been transformed out of all recognition. Lord's was no longer a country meadow but an amphitheatre for the great game. MCC was no longer just a private club – it was an institution. And as cricket entered the 20th century, MCC had become the administrative leader of world cricket, and Lord's was a ground that could proudly lead the game into its Golden Age.

War and Peace

In 1914 Lord's cricket ground celebrated its centenary in St John's Wood and a special match bill was produced to commemorate this milestone. As war clouds gathered over Europe, there was to be no more cricket of any consequence at Lord's for some time. In 1917, however, the Ground was used for a baseball match between the Canadians and London Americans in aid of a fund that helped the widows and orphans of Canadians who fell in battle.

In 1923 the Grace Gate was erected in memory of 'the Great Cricketer', and in 1926 the second Grand Stand was built. The architect of both was Sir Herbert Baker, who also presented MCC with the Father Time weather vane, which has since become a proud symbol of Lord's.

On the pitch William Ward's record score of 278, made in 1820, was passed twice in successive years: in 1925 Percy Holmes (Yorkshire) made 315 not out and the following year Jack Hobbs (Surrey) made 316 not out, which remained the ground record for the next 64 years.

One of the great names in the history of Lord's is that of Sir George 'Gubby' Allen. Playing for Middlesex v Lancashire in 1929 Allen took all ten wickets in an innings – the only time that this feat

The first team from the West Indies to tour England, 1900.
Back row: MM Kerr, SW Sproston, GL Livingston, PJ Cox, WC Nock, TB Burton, LS D'Ade, CA Ollivierre.
Middle row: WS Bowring, GC Learmond, RSA Warner (captain), PA Goodman, LS Constantine.
Front row: FS Hinds, S Woods. Warner was the brother of Sir Pelham Warner. Lebrun Constantine was the father of the great West Indian all-rounder Learie (later Lord) Constantine.

has been performed in a county match at Lord's.

The great Australian batsman Don Bradman heralded the 1930s by scoring 254 in his first Test on the ground in one of the finest matches of all time. The decade also saw the arrival of Len Hutton, the departure of Patsy Hendren and the heyday of Wally Hammond. In 1938 the England v Australia Test match was the first to be televised.

There was much more cricket in the Second World War (1939–45) than the First, and Lord's escaped virtually unscathed, the only casualty being Father Time, who suffered minor injuries. During the war the Ground was used as a reception centre for members of RAF Air Crew. The lives given by many of these brave men are commemorated in a plaque on the south side of the Pavilion.

Bill Edrich and Denis Compton walk out to bat during their record-breaking summer of 1947.

The second Grand Stand, opened in 1926. The architect was Sir Herbert Baker, also responsible for the Union Buildings in Pretoria and for designing (with Edwin Lutyens) New Delhi.

The ground also had a near miss in 1944 when a flying bomb passed over Lord's. The players threw themselves on the pitch. When play resumed, Jack Robertson, playing for the Army against the RAF, hit the next ball but one for a six.

Highlights of the immediate post-war years were the Victory Tests of 1945 – in one match a combined total of 90,000 spectators packed the Ground – and the golden summer of 1947, which saw Bill Edrich and Denis Compton delight the crowds day after day as they both passed the record for the number of runs scored by a batsman in an English season.

In the 1950 Lord's Test, West Indies won their first victory in

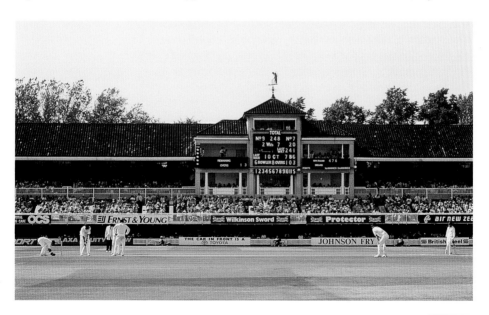

England in a match famous for the bowling of the West Indian spinners Sonny Ramadhin and Alf Valentine. Other developments at Lord's in the 1950s included the opening of the MCC Museum (1953) and the Warner Stand, built in 1958 on the site of the old 'A' enclosure.

Garry (later Sir Garfield) Sobers toasts the Lord's crowd at the end of his final Test match in England in 1973. Sobers scored an unbeaten 150 and West Indies won by an innings and 226 runs.

Revolution and Renewal

The early 1960s were notable for big changes in the game. In 1962 amateur status was abolished, and in that year a large crowd witnessed the last Gentlemen v Players match. The following year one-day cricket arrived in the form of the Gillette Cup, the first ever knockout competition. The annual final at Lord's, sponsored since 2006 by Friends Provident, is the climax of the county cricketing year.

A famous Lord's landmark disappeared in 1967 when the Tavern was pulled down to make way for a new stand. In 1969, amid the controversy of whether South Africa should be excluded from Test cricket, overall control of the game passed to a new body called the Cricket Council, consisting of MCC, the Test and County Cricket Board and the National Cricket Association.

In June 1975, Lord's played host to the first ever World Cup competition. In a tense final, West Indies beat Australia by 17 runs. The West Indies also won the 1979 competition, but were beaten in 1983 by India. That evening St John's Wood echoed with the celebrations of jubilant Indian supporters; India's triumph kick-started the country's long-running passion for the one-day game. The Prudential Trophy, awarded for these first three World Cup

Teams led by Greg Chappell (Australia) and Ian Botham (England) assemble for a group photograph of Test players past and present at the 1980 Centenary Test at Lord's between England and Australia, marking 100 years since the first Test match in England.

Two greats from the subcontinent batting for the same side at Lord's: Imran Khan (Pakistan) and Sunil Gavaskar (India) during a partnership of 180 for the Rest of the World XI against MCC in the Club's bicentenary match, August 1987.

competitions, is on display in the MCC Museum.

In 1977 Gubby Allen opened MCC's first Indoor School – intended, as the inscription by the entrance to the school states, to help 'cricketers of every age and ability'.

MCC celebrated its bicentenary in 1987. Many festivities were held, culminating in a great banquet at London's Guildhall and a spectacular match between MCC and the Rest of the World. Gordon Greenidge, Graham Gooch, Mike Gatting and Sunil Gavaskar all made centuries. The year was also notable for the completion of the much-acclaimed Mound Stand.

The last decade of the millennium brought more milestones. In 1990 Graham Gooch set a new ground record when he scored 333 in a Test match against India. The same year, the centenary of the Pavilion was celebrated with the establishment of the Lord's Tour, allowing many more people to see the Ground and view MCC's treasures. South Africa returned to the Test arena and on their first appearance back at Lord's in 1994 defeated England by 356 runs. Pakistan and New Zealand also achieved their first Test victories at Lord's. During the 1990s the skyline of Lord's changed dramatically with a number of fine additions to the architecture of the Ground. The Compton and Edrich Stands (1991), a new Indoor School (1995), a new Grand Stand (1998) and the remarkable Media Centre (1999) all contribute towards its reputation as

Vice captain Charlotte Edwards holds aloft the Ashes at Lord's as England Women take the applause for their 1–0 series defeat of Australia Women in 2005 – two weeks before their male counterparts won their Ashes. Caroline Atkins, a product of the MCC Young Cricketers programme, is at far right.

the world's finest cricket ground. The Media Centre was completed in time for the return of the World Cup Final in 1999, in which Australia beat Pakistan.

Off the pitch, cricket's governing bodies combined in 1997 to form the England and Wales Cricket Board (ECB), and in 1998 MCC voted to admit women as Members of the Club.

In 2000 Lord's celebrated its 100th Test Match, a game between England and West Indies, which turned out to be one of the most remarkable ever staged at the Ground. On the second day wickets fell with amazing regularity and, even though the day was interrupted by rain, parts of all four innings were played. The next day was equally exciting and, up until almost the very last ball, all four results were possible, but England finally won by two wickets.

The opening years of the 21st century also witnessed the first Test appearances at Lord's by Zimbabwe (2000) and Bangladesh (2005), while in 2005 MCC bade farewell to the ICC, who moved their operations to Dubai after being based at Lord's for almost 100 years.

The highlight of 2005, however, was the reopening of the

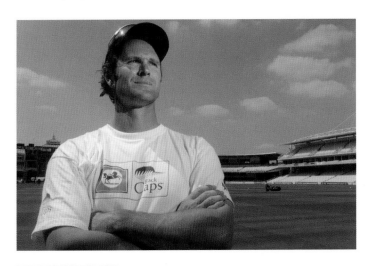

Chris Cairns, the New Zealand all-rounder who, in scoring 82 in the Lord's Test in May 2004, struck his 85th six in Test cricket, breaking the world record. His record is now held by Adam Gilchrist, who finished his career with 100 sixes.

Andrew Flintoff calls for a new bat after breaking one attempting to drive Makhaya Ntini during his innings of 142, made in defeat against South Africa at Lord's in 2003.

refurbished Pavilion – the oldest building at Lord's and one that has come to symbolise MCC and cricket worldwide. It is hoped that the Pavilion will continue to watch over the progress of MCC and cricket for at least another century.

Over the centuries much has altered at Lord's and much, quite rightly, will continue to change. But the essential nature of the place remains the same. We hope that Thomas Lord would feel at home if he were to come back to the Ground today, for Lord's is eternal in its appeal to all cricketers and cricket-lovers.

Andrew Strauss, the new England captain, at Lord's.

A Tour

The Grace Gate

When embarking on a tour of Lord's visitors normally enter through the Grace Gate, erected in 1923 as a memorial to Dr WG Grace (1848–1915), 'the Great Cricketer', one of England's first national sporting characters. The gate was designed by Sir Herbert Baker and is a fine example of Bromsgrove ironwork.

William Gilbert Grace was one of five brothers (three of whom played cricket for England), all taught the game by their mother Martha at the family home in Downend, Bristol. He was a natural athlete, tall and strong and possessed of great physical energy and an unquenchable appetite for his chosen sport.

WG Grace, photographed in 1874 at the age of 25.

A 1905 portrait of WG Grace by HS Tuke. The portrait was donated in its original frame by GW Beldam, the great cricket photographer, who was himself drawn by Tuke.

The Investec Media Centre stands between the Edrich (in the foreground) and Compton (background) stands.

He burst onto the cricket scene at a young age – he made his first century for South Wales against the Gentlemen of Sussex aged only 15 – and was to dominate the game for almost 40 years, by which time he had come to epitomise the image of Victorian sporting manhood.

He first came to notice at Lord's in 1868 when, aged 19, he scored his brilliant century for the Gentlemen against the Players. In 1871 he became the first cricketer ever to reach 2,000 runs in a season, and in 1873 was the first to achieve the double of 1,000 runs and 100 wickets in a season, a feat he achieved each year until 1878 and again twice in the 1880s. In 1876 he made 344 for MCC against Kent at Canterbury and followed this with scores of 177 against Notting-hamshire and 318 not out against Yorkshire the following week. He played in 22 Test matches against Australia, including the first Test played in England in 1880, in which he scored the first Test century in England.

He captained Gloucestershire for 25 years, leading the side twice to the County Championship. He also led England in 13 Test Matches between 1880 and 1899. His most famous season was 1895 when, at the age of 46, he became the first player to score 1,000 runs in May and hit his 100th first class century.

As well as being a great cricketer he was a larger-than-life character who was not averse to bending the Laws when it suited him. Many of the stories told about him refusing to walk when given out are true – he knew that people had come to see him bat!

Statue of WG Grace in the Coronation Gardens, with the Club's Thomas Lord roller in the background.

His last great season was 1898, but he continued to make occasional first-class appearances until 1908, his 60th year. He died of a heart attack, only seven years later, following an air-raid over London.

'WG' remains, 150 years after his birth, one of the most famous of all cricketers and is still instantly recognised by cricket followers the world over. Some have questioned whether he would be able to compete in today's modern game, but most agree that his is a remarkable record for a remarkable man. His career spanned two eras – when WG started over-arm bowling had only just been legalised – and it is certainly worth remembering that many of his best scores were made on pitches that would be considered extremely dangerous, if not unplayable, these days. It is unlikely that cricket will ever see his like again. Only one man, Sir Donald Bradman of Australia, has made an impact on the game that might be seen as comparable.

Around the Ground

On the right of the gate is the Allen Stand. Designed by Sir Herbert Baker and opened in 1934, it was refurbished and renamed in 1989 as a tribute to the Middlesex and England cricketer Sir George Allen (1902–1989). After his playing days were over, Gubby served as Treasurer of MCC from 1965 to 1976. On days when the county are playing at Lord's, the Middlesex Room in the lower part of the stand is used as clubroom by county members.

Lord Harris (1851–1932), painted by Arthur Hacker, RA.

Opposite the Allen Stand is the Harris Garden. Originally the site of a Lawn Tennis court, the garden was laid out in 1934 in memory of the 4th Lord Harris (1851–1932) who combined a notable cricketing career (Eton, Oxford, Kent and England) with distinguished public service. For half a century he was a predominant figure in the councils of the game, being MCC President in 1895 and Treasurer of the Club from 1916 to 1932. On most days the Harris Garden forms a quiet and restful retreat, but during Test matches it doubles as a hospitality area.

Beyond the Pavilion, moving clockwise around the Ground, you pass the Warner Stand. Sir Pelham 'Plum' Warner (1873–1963) was one of the great figures of Lord's. In 1899, then aged 15, he hit his first four at Lord's whilst playing for Rugby against Marlborough. His off-drive reached the boundary at extra-cover. It was at this place, some 60 years later, that Sir Pelham Warner

Sir Pelham 'Plum' Warner (1873–1963), in a posthumous portrait by Katherine Lloyd.

Panorama of the Ground from the Compton Stand.

became the first person to enter the new stand bearing his name. The stand, which dominates the south-west corner of the Ground, has seating for some 3,000 spectators, as well as a spacious bar and refreshment area providing an unrestricted view of the play. Even the lavatories have windows through which the occupants can keep apace of goings-on in the middle! The back of the Warner Stand looks out over the Coronation Garden, a popular

picnic spot on match days.

The Grand Stand on the west side of the Ground was designed by Nicholas Grimshaw and completed in 1998. This is the third stand on this site, replacing that designed by Baker in 1926. The stand, which was constructed entirely of pre-fabricated sections, has a lower terrace some 100 metres in length with a superstructure above that is supported on just three concrete columns. It holds 6,200 spectators and has 20 hospitality boxes. It was opened by HRH the Duke of Edinburgh on 18th June 1998 in time for the First Test against South Africa that season.

On the north side of the Ground, opposite the Pavilion, are the Compton and Edrich Stands, named after the two brilliant Middlesex and England batsmen Denis Compton (1918–1997) and Bill Edrich (1916–1986). Their golden season was the scorching summer of 1947 during which they each scored over 3,000 runs. The stands were completed in 1991 and opened by Denis Compton. Although plain in style, the stands are a great improvement on their predecessors which were very claustrophobic. The concrete work won a Concrete Society Award and the athletic structural design has given those seated on the lower terraces a much-improved view of play. MCC made the conscious decision not to build the stands any higher as it was felt important that the Ground should retain its intimate atmosphere and not be turned into a stadium.

Situated in the gap between these stands is the award-winning

View from the Mound Stand showing, from the left, the Pavilion, Warner Stand, Grand Stand, and the Compton and Edrich stands with the Media Centre in between.

A packed Mound Stand. Beyond, Father Time is perched on top of the lift shaft between the Mound and Tavern stands.

Media Centre, opened in 1999. Designed by Future Systems, it is the world's first all-aluminium semi-monocoque structure. The Media Centre is home to some 200 journalists and broadcasters who use its state-of-the-art technology to transmit the game to cricket followers worldwide.

On the east side of the Ground is the Mound Stand, rebuilt and opened in 1987 to commemorate the bicentenary of MCC. Greatly facilitated by a most generous gift from Sir Paul Getty, KBE, the stand was designed by Sir Michael Hopkins and has received many accolades from the architectural world. Its structure – employing a PVC-coated canopy – resembles the tents and marquees of a village cricket ground. The original terrace of the old Mound Stand (best viewed from the rear) was retained, and two further levels added, containing private boxes and viewing facilities.

In the south-west corner of the Ground is the Tavern Stand, originally the site of the much-loved Lord's Tavern. Controversially, this was demolished in 1967 to make way for the new complex with its popular bar and hospitality boxes. The Tavern was rebuilt to the west of the Grace Gate, together with a banqueting suite which provides spacious accommodation and modern facilities for the many conferences and other functions that take place at Lord's. The Tavern was fully refurbished and re-opened as the Lord's Tavern Bar and Brasserie in 2004. Guests of the Lord's Tour are welcome to pay a visit after their tour for some refreshment.

The Investec Media Centre (right) in October 2008. In the foreground is the Edrich Stand.

The Pavilion: the Cathedral of Cricket

The Pavilion at Lord's is one of the most celebrated buildings in the sporting world. A fine example of Victorian architecture, it is the third pavilion to stand on this site. The original pavilion, built by Thomas Lord, was burned down following a fixture between Eton and Harrow in 1825. The second, erected in time for the MCC anniversary dinner the following year, was a utilitarian construction that had, by the 1880s, undergone numerous additions and alterations. The MCC Committee agreed that it was time to build a new Pavilion more suitable for a club growing both in membership and international importance.

Designed by the architect Thomas Verity, the Pavilion was constructed in the winter of 1889–90 at a cost of £21,000. It was built to serve a membership of 4,000 and continues to fulfil many of its original functions, with not only changing and treatment rooms but also bars, lounges and cloakrooms, together with offices for a greatly-increased administrative staff.

During the winter of 2004–05 the Pavilion underwent a £7 million refurbishment which aimed to restore and conserve some of the important original features of the building as well as providing much improved facilities for Members (in 2005 numbering some 22,000), players, staff and public.

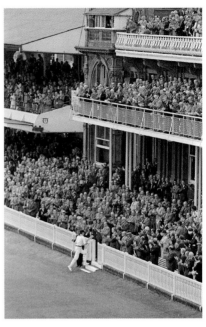

Greg Chappell receives a standing ovation from the Pavilion after making 131 against England in 1972.

Wide view of the Pavilion taken during the 1999 England v New Zealand Test match.

The Long Room, after the restoration of 2004–05.

For most cricket enthusiasts the highlight of the Lord's Tour is a visit to the famous Long Room. Measuring 90ft (27m) in length, the room offers a magnificent view of the playing area, acts as a clubroom for MCC Members, and provides a stunning backdrop for dinners and other events.

Either side of the Long Room are two other fine rooms, the Writing Room and the Committee Room, where many of cricket's most important decisions have been made. All three rooms provide a perfect setting for many of MCC's important works of art – landscapes of cricket dating back to the 18th century and portraits of many of the game's most famous players and administrators.

The first floor houses the dressing rooms for players and Members. The players' quarters are situated in the towers at either end of the building. The home side (which, depending on the match, might be England, Middlesex or MCC) uses the south tower nearer the Grace Gate; the visitors use the north tower. The players walk down the stairs and through the Long Room on their way to and from the pitch.

The top floor houses the players' and Committee dining rooms and a Members' lounge. One innovation is a roof-terrace from where, on match days, Members can enjoy the sun, a drink and an unrivalled view of the cricket.

Now given a Grade II listing, the Pavilion at Lord's has served as a model for other sports pavilions all over the world, including those at the Oval and Old Trafford.

The Writing Room. The painting of Lord's over the fireplace is by William Bowyer RA, which was commissioned to celebrate the bicentenary of MCC in 1987. On the wall to the right hangs *An Imaginary Cricket Match: England v Australia at Lord's* by Barrable and Ponsonby Staples, 1887.

Sir Ian Botham and Andrew Flintoff in 2007, at a reception held in the Long Room following the investiture ceremony for Botham's knighthood. Botham holds the record for the most Test wickets (69) at Lord's; he also scored 652 runs here. In 1978 he scored a century and took 8 for 34 in a Lord's Test against Pakistan.

View from the Pavilion's new roof-terrace.

Real Tennis: the Game of Kings

The game of Tennis can be traced back to the 13th century. It has recently become known as Real Tennis to distinguish itself from the modern game of Lawn Tennis. The game had its origins in medieval Europe, and the eccentric shape of the court, with its complicated grilles and galleries, is said to derive from the contours of monastic cloisters where the game was played. Terms still in use, such as *dedans, grille* and *tambour*, point to it being French in origin, although the first book on the game, *Il Trattato della Palla (The Treatise of the Ball)* was published in Venice in 1555.

Over many centuries it was the favourite sport of French and English kings. Henry VII and Henry VIII were both keen players and the latter built several courts, including one at Hampton Court that is still in use today. Many people first heard of the game from

The Australian Rob Fahey in action at Lord's. Fahey is the reigning Real Tennis world champion, who has defended his title a record eight times since first winning it in 1994.

HRH the Earl of Wessex presenting the trophy for the 2008 Real Tennis European Open, held at MCC, to the American player, Camden Riviere (left), who is currently the world number two.

Shakespeare, who mentions it in no fewer than five of his plays. Today, His Royal Highness the Earl of Wessex is a keen Real Tennis player and he has played on the court at Lord's on a number of occasions.

Lord's possesses one of only about 20 Real Tennis courts in the country. Its first court was built on the site of what is now the Mound Stand in 1838. The present court was opened on 1st January 1900. To the uninitiated the game makes for strange viewing. The racket, which originally derived its shape from the palm of the hand with which the ball was struck, has remained largely unchanged for the last 200 years. (In France the game is known as *Jeu de Paume*.) The ball has a hard centre with a soft felt cover and has less bounce than a Lawn Tennis ball. Spectators of the game are immediately struck by the considerable skill shown by the competitors. The game combines physical activity with considerable subtlety and, because of this latter quality, can be played to a high standard at an age beyond most other racket games.

The Lord's Tavern

Eating and drinking have long been an integral part of a day at the cricket. From a village tea to a grand dinner given in honour of the touring team, the catering arrangements often involve as much care and attention as the match itself. Indeed it could be argued that cricket remains the only sporting event whose timings are dictated by the ceremonies of taking meals.

Many of the earliest recorded matches were sponsored by local taverns. They would recoup their outlay by charging for lunch, and in the sale of large quantities of alcohol that seem to have been consumed not only after but during the match. Indeed we only know of the existence of some of these matches because of the subsequent court reports resulting from what could sometimes amount to riotous behaviour. It is no wonder that the Puritans did their best to put a stop to cricket altogether.

Thomas Lord, a wine-merchant himself, was well aware of the need to supply refreshment and there was a tavern on the first Lord's Ground at Dorset Fields. Not only that, but Lord opened a wine shop abutting the ground, through which all spectators had to pass in order to reach the field of play. With all his high-class

Hambledon, the leading 18th century cricket club in the days before MCC was formed, grew up around a local tavern, the Bat and Ball Inn, depicted here in an 1879 painting by CP Gale.

Huge crowds in front of the Tavern Stand in around 1950.

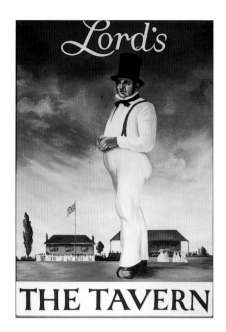

This sign for the Lord's Tavern, in the Museum collection, depicts Alfred Mynn, 'the Lion of Kent', a great player of the early 19th century. Thomas Lord is featured on the sign's other side.

The modern day Tavern Stand, which replaced its predecessor in 1967.

patrons it was not long before Lord was supplying wine to the finest society tables. There can be little doubt that he made far more money from his wine business than he did from his ownership of Lord's.

In October 1867 the Committee appointed architects Paraire and Co. to design a new tavern and hotel complex, which was completed for just under £4,000. MCC was delighted with its new facility, which afforded a double entrance to the Ground as well as providing extra seating for spectators.

The Tavern became a much-loved Lord's venue. The boxes, with their charming wrought-iron balustrades, were honoured by the presence of royalty and prime ministers and some of the most illustrious figures in the Commonwealth. However, the facilities of the 100-year old building could no longer cater to more modern needs and, after a lot of heart-searching, MCC decided to completely redevelop the south-west corner of the Ground. The old Tavern and hotel buildings were demolished in 1967 and in their place was erected a modern four-tier stand designed by Kenneth Peacock. To the left of the Grace Gate a banqueting suite was built, and facing onto St John's Wood Road a new tavern was opened. Both continue to offer a wide range of year-round dining opportunities, which are complemented on match days by mobile food and drink outlets. Eating and drinking remain an important part of a day at the cricket.

The Father Time Weather Vane

The Father Time weather vane, which has become such a well-known Lord's symbol, was a gift to MCC from Sir Herbert Baker, the architect of the second Grand Stand, which was completed in 1926 and demolished in 1996. It was a complete surprise to the MCC Committee, no member of which had any prior knowledge of the gift. It was intended to compensate MCC for the disquiet felt by the Club about the cost of the stand and its late completion, which was caused partly by the 1926 General Strike.

The figure represented is the mythical Father Time character (similar to the Roman god Janus after whom the month of January is named) who watches over the passage of time.

There has always been some debate in cricketing circles as to whether the figure depicted is placing the bails at the start of a game or removing them at the end of a day's play. Diana Rait Kerr, MCC's first curator, suggests that he is removing the bails. However, the cricket writer EW Swanton took the more optimistic view that the bails are being placed in anticipation of a day's cricket.

The weather vane is around 6ft 6in (2m) in total, although the

Father Time figure itself measures approximately 5ft 4in (1.7m). It is made of cast iron, which is painted black, with gilding on the tip of the wind-arrow and the end of Father Time's sickle.

Father Time was the only casualty of the Second World War at Lord's when the cables of a drifting barrage balloon became entangled with the weather vane which was wrenched from the top of the Grand Stand and deposited on the seats below. He spent the remainder of the War housed safely in the Committee Room.

Early in 1992 the weather vane was struck by lightning during a thunderstorm. Father Time's hand had to be replaced and the entire weather vane was repaired, repainted and regilded by the MCC Works Department. It was during this period that Father Time took his only trip away from Lord's when he made a special appearance on the BBC children's programme *Blue Peter* on 20th February 1992.

When Sir Herbert Baker's Grand Stand was demolished, Father Time was moved to his new home on top of the lift shaft between the Mound and Tavern stands. From this new position Father Time continues to watch over Lord's into the 21st century.

When the new Grand Stand was built in 1998, Father Time was moved (above) from its perch on the old Grand Stand to its new location crowning the lift shaft at the south-west end of the Mound Stand.

The Playing Area

According to tradition, each time Thomas Lord moved his ground he took the turf with him. Whether or not this is correct, cricketers have always liked to imagine that they are treading in the footsteps of their illustrious predecessors. The playing area at Lord's, however, has always been somewhat problematic; cricketers over the years have had to accept its little idiosyncrasies, such as the slope, which measures an approximate 6ft 6in (2m) drop from the Warner to the Tavern Stand.

A more serious problem arose from the fact that the soil underlying the turf was largely composed of London clay – a dense material that saturates very quickly and drains poorly. Over the years many hours of cricket were lost because of pools of water remaining on the surface long after any rain had stopped.

Between September 2002 and March 2003, in the largest project ever undertaken on the playing surface at Lord's, the entire main ground – except for the playing square – was dug out and re-laid. In a project costing £1.25 million, some 20,000 tons of heavy clay soil was removed. Deep drains and state-of-the-art sprinkler systems were laid and the ground level was rebuilt with various layers of coarse gravel and fine sand designed to ensure good drainage. This was topped with a specially selected turf that had been grown off-site and transported in rolls to Lord's.

Lord's, now considered to be a very good wicket, long had a reputation for its difficult pitch, as observed here by Roy Ullyett (1914–2001), the greatest sports cartoonist of his generation.

The outfield being dug up and relaid during the 2002–03 close season. It now drains remarkably well, enabling play to restart quickly after rain. The famous slope runs downhill from left to right in this picture.

Groundsman at work. Behind are the Mound and Tavern stands, between which are the new scorers' box and the lift shaft, with Father Time up above.

MCC had its share of good luck. The winter was mild, thus ensuring that work progressed on schedule and the fine new playing surface was ready for the start of the 2003 season. It has so far proved a great success and MCC has achieved its goal of providing the maximum opportunities to play cricket at Lord's in the best possible conditions.

And what of the old turf? This was packaged and sold off, in bulk to Members and in smaller quantities to the public, raising around £35,000 towards the project. A certain amount was retained and made into paperweights so that visitors to Lord's can continue to purchase a piece of Lord's original turf in the MCC Shop.

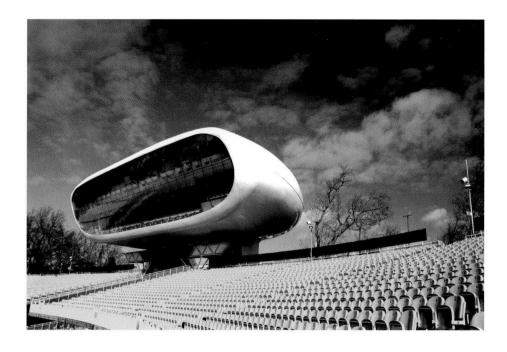

The Investec Media Centre

The Investec Media Centre at Lord's, built in time for the 1999 ICC Cricket World Cup, was the first all-aluminium semi-monocoque building in the world. Designed by Future Systems Limited and costing £5.8 million, its construction was truly innovative – it was built and fitted out not by the construction industry but by a boatyard using the very latest advances in boat-building technology.

The centre stands 49ft (15m) above the ground, with access via lifts incorporated into the supports of the building. The main body of the building consists of a large pod which was constructed in two parts (one in a shipbuilder's yard in Falmouth, the other in Holland), then assembled and welded together on site. The front wall comprises one single pane of glass and, in a remarkable feat of engineering, all components fitted together exactly. The split-level interior is fitted out in a soft blue colour which was chosen so that, when seen from outside through the glass wall, its appearance would be neutral and not distract the players. There is a distinctly nautical feeling to the whole inside which is enhanced by the very high standard of finish usually associated with yacht building. The overall effect of interior with exterior is visually spectacular.

On big match days the Investec Media Centre is very much the hub of media activity. The lower tier of the building provides

Cleaners at work on the outside of the Media Centre. Cleaning takes place once every season.

seating to over 100 journalists and cricket writers, each with telephone and internet access, TV monitors and an unrivalled view of the playing area. Spiral staircases lead up to a gallery where television and radio crews are housed in separate studios for both

The Media Centre full with journalists on a big match day.

commentary and 'in-vision' presentations. To the rear of the centre a bar and restaurant area caters for the needs of all working media, and a photographers' suite offers facilities for images to be sent directly to newspapers and other publications as the action unfolds.

On non-match days the building is adapted for use as a conference centre or dining room and it has also been used as a location for advertisements and a pop video.

Numerous construction and design awards have been given to this outstanding building which is surely becoming as much an icon of Lord's as the Pavilion. The highest accolade was the award of the 1999 RIBA Stirling Prize for Architecture – the premier award in its field.

The Nursery End

Behind the Media Centre is the area known as the Nursery End. Many people assume that the term 'nursery' in a cricket context means a cradle for the development of young cricketers. The truth is more fanciful.

In the early years of Lord's, MCC Members had been allowed to practise archery on an area adjoining the Ground which was owned by Henderson's Nursery, famed for the quality of its tulips and pineapples. In 1887, to celebrate the Club's centenary, MCC bought the whole area of 3.5 acres (1.4 hectares) and converted it into a practice area for cricket. It was surrounded by a chain of graceful arbours that were in great demand on social occasions such as the Eton v Harrow match.

The Nursery Ground, although small, is adequate in size to act as home to the Cross Arrows Cricket Club (the Lord's 'domestic' team comprising MCC staff and Members) which plays matches there each September.

Currently on the Nursery Ground MCC is experimenting with three drop-in pitches similar to those used at the Sydney and Melbourne Cricket Grounds. The use of drop-in pitches on the main square would allow more matches to be played and would also enable MCC to host other non-cricketing events such as concerts without damaging the wicket.

The Nursery is also used as a site for practice nets and the Nursery pavilion provides a year-round hospitality facility.

Facing on to the Nursery Ground is the MCC Indoor School.

View of the Nursery Ground, with the Indoor School beyond and the Nursery Pavilion to the right.

An experimental drop-in pitch on the Nursery Ground.

It was designed by David Morley and opened in 1998, replacing the original school built in 1977. MCC has a long tradition of promoting youth cricket and the school is where the Lord's Easter Classes, instituted by Sir Francis Lacey in 1902, take place. Today it has state-of-the-art facilities, with a video analysis suite including the latest Hawk-Eye technology. In the social areas, photographs of great players past and present provide an added stimulus for aspiring young cricketers. Spectators have a splendid view of the cricket hall from the gallery on the first floor that runs the length of the nets. Behind this is a bar that overlooks the Nursery and a fully equipped modern gymnasium. The Indoor School's excellent facilities are available to clubs and individuals as well as Members of MCC. The MCC Indoor School has long been regarded as one of the finest cricket coaching venues in the world and has produced some of the game's finest cricketers such as Sir Ian Botham, Martin Crowe and Angus Fraser.